MARQUEE SUPERVISION

——— WITH ———

PURPOSE

MARQUEE
SUPERVISION
—— WITH ——
PURPOSE

HOW TO COACH, LEAD, AND INVEST
IN THE MODERN EMPLOYEE
AND ESTABLISH A CULTURE
OF PROFESSIONALISM
AND ACCOUNTABILITY

DR. CHARLES I. BROWN JR.

ISBN: 978-1-7366798-0-7 (paperback)
ISBN: 978-1-7366798-1-4 (hardcover)
ISBN: 978-1-7366798-2-1 (e-book)

Although this publication is designed to provide accurate information
in regard to the subject matter covered, the publisher and the author
assume no responsibility for errors, inaccuracies, omissions, or any other
inconsistencies herein. This publication is meant as a source of valuable
information for the reader, however it is not meant as a replacement for
direct expert assistance. If such level of assistance is required, the services
of a competent professional should be sought.

Editing by Tia Ross, TiaRossEditor.com
Book design by DTPerfect.com

Contact the author at:
marqueesupervision@gmail.com

TABLE OF CONTENTS

CHAPTER 3: ESTABLISHING PRACTICES
FOR BUSINESS LONGEVITY   61

INTRODUCTION

You will find tons of literature dedicated to the topic of management, and there are many more workshops, videos, and seminars available at your fingertips. However, they are mostly broad generalizations that fail to share specific practical remedies that matter. Most resources enable and relabel excuses, gradually taking the power and influence out of the hands of those in leadership positions. This book puts leadership and supervision back into the driver's seat for business success and shows the reader how to coach or expel those staff uninterested in being team players or adhering to the standards of professionalism established.

The truth is we spend more time with our co-workers than we do our families. The two worlds today are so connected that they become an extension of the other. Employees are logged in to social networks while at work, which meshes the "at-home" mindset with their workplace environment. Co-workers are also interacting with one another as they would with family and are handling work situations in a similar fashion. This is where I say enough is enough. Supervisors must redefine the workplace environment to clearly delineate and clarify boundaries to separate work from home.

It is important that all supervisors accept people's unpredictable nature and stay ready for the curve balls that may be thrown. Supervisors are most effective when they can identify the red flags of an issue brewing and address it before it fully manifests. If the lessons are practiced consistently, managers will no longer waste time and energy trying to influence or encourage staff to do their jobs and do them well. Supervisors will no longer have to play psychologist to inspire staff to complete the job expected of them at the level necessary. The customer can enter the business knowing they are highly valued and matter.

In Chapter 1, we will discuss the responsibilities and expectations of a manager or supervisor. You have the title, now you must play the part. This chapter lays a foundation for how you should act as a supervisor and teaches how you must interact with staff. This chapter will also discuss problem-solving steps and how best to approach different situations.

Chapter 2 will teach you how to build an ideal work environment. It will also discuss the responsibilities and expectations of your employees and reinforce many of the lessons discussed in Chapter 1. This chapter will clearly define the parameters conducive to a positive workplace environment and debunk the label of "bad employee."

Today's workplace has the tendency to tie the hands of those in charge and make it difficult for change to occur and progress to commence. Employees feel empowered to complain when things don't go their way or when they are required to put in an honest day's work. I say throw out the "bottom-up leadership" mumbo jumbo, retrain our employees, and hold them accountable for their actions.

Chapter 3 will teach you how to develop responsible team members and improve team morale. In this chapter, employees will adopt a unified goal and become self-governing. This chapter also speaks about important considerations for sustainability and expansion.

The ability to lead isn't an innate quality endowed by a select few. It is a skill learned by experience and practice. This book is written for anyone aiming to build a positive, productive, and professional workplace environment. It will teach the reader steps to problem solving and share specific remedies for handling adverse situations.

CHAPTER 1

ESTABLISHING SELF

Over 30 million small businesses operating within the United States account for almost half of the US workforce and employ over 60 million people.[1] Small businesses play a vital role in the US and global economies, and their ingenuity and success provide a plethora of opportunities for employees to explore and secure positions that meet their current individual needs. In climates of high job availability, small businesses are competing to attract and retain the best available talent through unique benefit packages. However, these packages cannot offer insight into the type of workplace environment that exists without them actually being experienced. The general

---

1 "U.S. Small Business Economic Profile." *Small Business Administration*, SBA Office of Advocacy, 2020, cdn.advocacy.sba.gov/wp-content/uploads/2020/06/04144224/2020-Small-Business-Economic-Profile-US.pdf.

atmosphere of a business is as important a recruitment tool as the other benefits being offered.

Candidates are normally skeptical of the "perfect environment" and "family atmosphere" often presented during their official visits. These environments are established by the owner and propagated by the supervisor they hire to execute the mission. One can gather great insight into a business and discern its true nature by observing their turnover rate and learning how long current employees have been there. Employees are more likely to remain with a single business for the entirety of their careers if they enjoy their workplace environment, support the mission of the business, and are content with the benefits they receive. There isn't a lot that can lure this employee away; however, any change in happiness can lead them out the door in search of better opportunities.

Two of the many responsibilities of a supervisor are to keep employees feeling valued and to maintain a professional and nontoxic work environment. Businesses rely on employees to complete the two very important tasks of efficiently producing a quality product or service and representing the business admirably to the customer. The supervisor guides and coaches the employee(s) toward success and weeds out those that antagonize the business's mission and negatively influence public opinion.

Supervision failures often result in poor working environments with ethically poor staff, unstable and unreliable business practices, and poor morale with employee distrust. For new or first-time supervisors, it is important they understand that supervision is a developmental process which requires mental fortitude, focus, and consistency. A supervisor's goal is to execute the mission of the business and train staff to optimally perform. They must lead by example and encourage their staffs to consistently offer top-notch customer service, work diligently, and avoid unnecessary waste. Businesses thrive when supervision is done correctly. On the other hand, supervisors must avoid being irresolute, dishonest, unfair, inconsistent, and poor team players. Possession of any of these shortcomings will lead to immense failure and, ultimately, business losses. Businesses composed of winning teams have unlimited potential, are able to withstand unpredictable setbacks without having to make unwanted sacrifices or endure significant financial loss, and they have employees that are generally happy, responsible, and reliable.

A supervisor's journey must begin by dealing with the issues of self and establishing a strong internal foundation that will allow them to be an effective leader. Being a good supervisor takes hard work, discipline, and practice. Also, no one can supervise staff effectively without the proper confidence, direction, and knowledge. Good supervisors understand how to operate within what is reality and are able to identify and focus on the variables within their control without getting lost and misguided by false realities and the highly unlikely images of perfection carried in their minds.

As employees climb the career ladder and assume various leadership positions, most are deservingly excited with assuming their first supervisorial role. What's unfortunate is that most neither realize nor are willing to admit that they are inadequately prepared to meet the full demands of the position. Subsequent experiences will soon quell their excitement, and their ingenuous ambition will quickly dissolve as reality sets in and new challenges commence. These challenges will be great character builders and will present new growth opportunities. This is often a painful and stressful process, but this book will help prepare the supervisor to successfully address issues of inherited failed business practices, poor workplace culture and environment, and poorly coached staff.

Supervision does not require unique psychological and manipulative ability to persuade and encourage the employee to complete the job expected of them. Supervision requires constant vigilance and the knowledge that the employee doesn't dictate what is or isn't done. A poorly coached employee can easily exploit the inexperienced supervisor, and the last thing a business needs is for a rattled supervisor to lose both control of the workplace environment and focus on the mission and current goals. Such outcomes will result in a toxic working environment, which will create unnecessary and negative internal noise for each team member that they will each manifest and express differently.

Internal noise is a form of mental anguish that will cause some staff to suffer from dejection, falter in their decision-making, and ultimately withdraw from any concern and interest in the business's success and their contributions to it. Unfortunately, these internal noise stresses don't dissipate once one leaves work; it has the potential to adversely affect other aspects of one's life, such as sleep and familial relationships. Any employee of the business subject to a sleepless night due to this stress is one too many, and the supervisor must be prepared and have the know-how for remedying these unexpected and sometimes challenging situations involving staff.

When establishing a strong foundation of self, first know which characteristics and behaviors make a good supervisor. A supervisor must first always exude confidence no matter the situation and set the tone for the environment for which all must work. Also, the supervisor must never be guilty of any accusation they make toward others, engage in gossip, nor lose their cool. Supervisors must always perform in the manner expected of them, exude positivity and professionalism, and never compromise their integrity.

Supervisorial positions are attained in various ways and, once assumed, it is important to become passionate and dedicated to the responsibilities of the position. The role isn't always fun, and sometimes supervisors have to make decisions that are unpopular. During these times, the supervisor must always remember to do what is right without having to seek the validation of others in an effort to please and make them feel comfortable. Doing what's right will always yield the most successful outcomes for the business in the long run. Those that are unable to make tough decisions and have difficulty fulfilling the requirements of the position are most likely to have their days numbered with the business.

Supervisors must also avoid cutting corners when completing tasks because it will eventually lead to their having to repeat the initial steps all over again from doing it incorrectly the first time. Unnecessary repetition due to poor business practices leads to wasted time and resources.

Observant staff will always be aware of how supervisors lead and perform so that they may use it as excuse to justify any of their poor future behaviors. Employees learn how to conduct themselves based on the example set by their supervisor. For example, if you speak ill of your supervisor, then expect your staff to speak ill of you. If you come in late, then expect the tardiness of your staff to increase. Have pride in your work and all that you do and never regress to less than what you would expect from your team. If you practice going the extra mile, then your staff will understand your expectations and not be surprised with additional duties and requests.

Good supervisors also complete needed tasks without having to be told by their superiors. They never put things off to the last minute, then rush to complete, causing unnecessary stress and frustration to their team. They do not run from conflict or avoid tough conversations by cowering in their office. Any avoidance of team interaction is counterintuitive to teamwork and will ultimately have adverse effects on team morale and produce fragmentation within the foundations you wish to establish for a positive workplace environment.

Supervisors must always be visible and accessible to their staff. With 40-hour or more workweeks, staff spends more quality time with one another than their actual families. In a sense, the business is their home away from home, and it is essential that supervisors help staff to foster their relationships with one another in a professional manner conducive to a positive work environment. This will require that supervisors be compassionate and have the ability to solve problems, communicate, and delegate. Your goal is to build a team with sustainable practices that support the mission and goals of the business. Investing in your team on an intangible level shows that you value the individual.

COMPASSION

All supervisors must lead with limited compassion due to their responsibilities to the business. Compassion is something that can be learned but not taught. Staff is delicate, no matter how tough they appear to be on the outside. As supervisor, you should have the mentality to serve others but not to the extent you begin losing your identity or sacrificing your responsibilities to those you have deemed to be the absolute priority in your life. Respect what you can do for others and be sure to never lead with sympathy. Being sympathetic will blindside you with unexpected and unfavorable results that will destabilize the foundations you wish to establish.

Compassion for the supervisor entails nonjudgmental listening if someone chooses to confide in you, offering needed support without seeking or receiving a benefit, and sacrificing your time to be there for someone when they need you. Compassion does not involve donating money, and you should never feel guilty about not supporting a cause financially if you do not feel like it. Sometimes, just listening is all that is required and will help immensely. Just remember that people aren't their usual selves during times of bereavement and other significantly stressful situations.

COMMUNICATION

Most people like to speak and be heard, but very few care to listen and communicate. The ability to communicate effectively is a vital part of any job, and it requires an adequate amount of attention, as would anything relevant. Unfortunately, it is easier for people to show their feelings through their attitudes and actions rather than use words to express themselves. When words are used, there is no guarantee that the listener will receive the message in the manner the supervisor wished it to be understood or interpreted. When communications break down, the results are often undesirable and may have minimal to severe impacts. Miscommunication-induced errors can sometimes be remedied with a simple fix, or they can result in serious situations that produce ill feelings and unforgivable actions. No matter their outcomes, the supervisor has the responsibility to rectify the situation.

When addressing any individual or a group, always make sure that your body language exudes the utmost confidence. When listening to someone speak, avoid using distractive gestures such as jerky hand movements, excessive head nods, uninterested head tilts, and facial expressions. Also avoid deep sighs, wandering eyes, smiling when inappropriate, and unwarranted laughing. When it's time to speak, do so in an audible tone, using only direct responses or commands to minimize the chances of misinterpretation. If you ever charge someone with being a poor communicator, then you're equally guilty if you aren't paraphrasing what is being said to improve your understanding. The likelihood of misinterpretation decreases when supervisors are consistent, transparent, and direct.

DELEGATING

Supervisors must be able to comfortably delegate responsibility to staff because it is impossible to do everything yourself. Delegation appropriately used can raise team morale and individual staff confidence. Delegate the most difficult or most important task to the person that would be best at completing it, and if that person is you, then make sure that you complete the task with someone under your wing to learn. Strive to put staff in positions for success. You want to build staff up so that small victories are a norm; they become independent and start taking the initiative to complete tasks without having to be asked or directed.

When delegating a task, respect and be patient with approaches different from your own. Your priority is to make sure that the goal is understood, waste and fraud are not being committed, and progress is being made in a timely fashion. Trust people to do what is asked of them with indirect observation and periodic updates. Avoid micromanaging or expecting the delegate to complete the task in the same manner as you. It is always possible to learn something new and possibly better if you trust your decision with the delegation.

If you are uncertain that the delegate knows how to complete a certain task, then ask them directly: "Do you know how to…?" If they answer in the affirmative, then allow them reasonable time to complete the task on their own without overbearing observance. In the event someone answers in the affirmative that they can complete a particular task and it is proven they could not, do not get upset. Make sure that they learn what it is you would like them to know. This simple act of teaching rather than scolding is one way to invest in staff and show that you value their contributions. The act also plants a seed of trust, which could garner future loyalty, support, and a higher level of work ethic. This employee investment also antagonizes the development and growth of any unknown team-destroying behaviors within the business and strengthens team cohesiveness and commitment.

SELF-CONTROL AND ANGER

Problems are inevitable, and the supervisor has the responsibility to solve them. No matter the problem, you must be able to control your emotions. It's okay to become upset but never okay to lose your cool and express uncontrollable anger. Not many people can address a situation effectively during times of anger because emotions can go from 0–10 faster than the speed of light. First, you must understand that staff will make errors, sometimes repeatedly. The results of these errors will vary in severity and the effect they have on the business. Depending on the supervisor, however, their level of anger and response can vary significantly. It is never okay to punish others with your uncontrollable anger. You must learn to practice patience and train yourself to cap the rage before you can act or respond to the stimulant. Uncontrollable anger is an individual shortcoming that is counterproductive and destabilizes the intrapersonal foundations that you are trying to build upon. When you have the urge to choke someone, practice various exit phrases so that you can get away and address the issue later with a calmer and cooler head in a professional manner. Having self-control speaks volumes of individual character, and it gives immense power and ability to solve problems beyond your own.

TEAMWORK

Teamwork begins with the supervisor leading by example, respecting their staff, and holding staff accountable. Teamwork is staff working together harmoniously in an environment in which they can rely upon their fellow staff to uphold their responsibilities, and they are cheerfully willing to step in and help if it is needed. Supervisors must establish a set of core values that dictate the behaviors and expectations of all staff. At a minimum, these core values should include honesty, dependability, positivity, compassion, and professionalism. Core values lay the foundations of teamwork and a professional work environment.

===

CHAPTER 2

ESTABLISHING GOALS
AND BOUNDARIES

O nce you have built a positive intrapersonal awareness, it is time to begin establishing a working environment that breeds winning teams and not private and antagonizing armies. According to *Forbes*, over 50% of people are unhappy with their jobs, and they aren't invested in the mission of the business nor concerned about matters that do not affect them directly.[2] These unhappy employees' only concern is to show up just enough to receive a paycheck and benefits and try to have fun at the expense of the business. Their sentiments and behaviors have resulted in an unfortunate culture shift in the workplace that is

---

2   Kelly, Jack. "More Than Half Of U.S. Workers Are Unhappy In Their Jobs: Here's Why And What Needs To Be Done Now." *Forbes*, Forbes Magazine, 25 Oct. 2019, www.forbes.com/sites/jackkelly/2019/10/25/more-than-half-of-us-workers-are-unhappy-in-their-jobs-heres-why-and-what-needs-to-be-done-now

fragmenting business stability, growth, and the morale of dedicated staff. Unhappy staff is pushing boundaries and breaking rules to better accommodate themselves, and businesses are propagating these detrimental practices through the unsuccessful addressing of staff concerns and their negative behavior. It is essential that staff is happy but not at the expense of the business, the services provided, and the customer.

Your goal as supervisor is to get the very best out of your staff every day and make sure that everyone has everything they need to get their job done to support the mission. Avoid catering to the unnecessary wants of staff because they are unending and will never be fulfilled. As businesses endure changes, so will staff desires. Appeasing staff's every demand will inadvertently create an environment with everyone wanting more for doing less.

EXCUSES

As a supervisor, you must be able to understand and quickly identify excuses. An excuse is any reason given as to why something cannot be done without a valid reason supporting or answering the "why not." When supervisors resort to using excuses, it is often due to the difficulty they have coming up with a meaningful solution or simply to avoid having to make a tough decision. Labels are a form of excuses that act as a coping mechanism to allow a fallacious peace of mind for an undetermined period, and they help to justify not handling a current problem promptly. For example, the term "difficult employee" is an employee label used to describe individuals that incite discord at a moment when you are unable to handle the situation effectively. Labels cannot remedy any situation and therefore are useless.

There is also the concept of "vacuuming," used to describe poor employee behavior following the departure of a beloved supervisor within the business. In this situation, once highly performing employees become unmotivated about their responsibilities and assume a skeptical and often uncommitted demeanor to the successor, which often leads to poorer job performance and other challenges. It is important for incoming supervisors to understand that they are responsible for establishing workplace culture and ensuring that staff is meeting the expectations of the business. The challenges of poor employee behaviors will only persist and escalate if the supervisor allows it to continue. Anyone who has performed exemplary for your predecessor can perform the same way with you, and his or her poor behaviors should never be tolerated or excused.

Ill-prepared supervisors and those lacking strong leadership foundations fail to realize that consistently poor staff behavior is enabled by their inability as supervisor to find a system of accountability that works for everyone. As a result of these weaknesses, supervisors are more apt to pursue fad managerial techniques or unabashedly turn to the use of misleading and unproven personality tests that often fail and lead to more excuses. It is important to know that all personality types commit infractions, and no one personality is more conducive to a positive and professional work environment than another. Treating any staff differently because of perceived personality will inherently create more dysfunction and discord for the business. Staff issues are unending and their solutions are to match. The best way to avoid feeling the necessity to use excuses is by strengthening your intrapersonal awareness and establishing strong supervisorial foundations.

Strong supervisorial foundations will prevent once "delusional" staff from undeservingly viewing themselves as exceptional and passing the hard work of others as their own. It will also create a harmonious work environment and discourage staff from frivolously challenging your authority due to known consequence. Supervisors must demand the best from all of their staff and understand that the use of labels won't improve poor staff behaviors. The failure of a supervisor to properly coach their staff is only an insight into their poor ability to lead. Don't make excuses for yourself or anyone else. Coach staff with consistency and fairness to yield desirable behaviors.

Know Your Job Description

Before you begin setting the tone for the workplace environment, it is essential to understand the full responsibilities of your position and the expectations of your superiors. Verify that you can execute the tasks of your job description and that you have complete autonomy over your division because not all "leadership" titles mean that you have real authority. You do not want outside entities from other divisions dictating what your staff can or cannot do and influencing the effectiveness of the operations for which you have responsibility. You want easy access to your budget, control of your schedule, knowledge of where your funding is coming from, if applicable, and what current collaborations and partnerships exist. You want to avoid taking blame for matters you do not have control over and allowing the shortcomings of others to tarnish your reputation. You were selected for the position because of your experience, expertise, and/ or additional training in an area. You must know and believe that you are the best person for the job and not allow those with limited knowledge of your division to dictate how you operate or convince you that their ideas are best against your own judgment. You want others to complete duties within their job descriptions and not attempt to overstep their boundaries to fulfill your responsibilities.

BUSINESS EXPECTATIONS AND MISSION

When coming into a business, understand that leadership has a responsibility to recruit the best talent to further their mission, and they may not always be forthcoming about their shortcomings and future aspirations. You want to know their mission and get in writing the specific goals and expectations they have for your division. Obtain specific numerical financial goals and performance goals expectant of your division, then compare these goals to your team's current production and performance and to those of the past five years. Senior leadership should share expectations like "Increase monthly production by 10%, Cut costs by 50,000, Complete 20 customer encounters per day, etc." You also want to know if the business is having financial issues surrounding your division and whether it is production-related or due to another factor, such as fewer grants received or an experienced hardship or catastrophe. Know the historic levels of staffing and correlate these changes with the fluctuations of financial performance during the corresponding period. Also, find out what advanced technological resources are available to the staff, and document when there have been periods of construction, equipment failure, illness, or inclement weather that may have influenced production. If a business increases its staff, it must also increase the resources available to staff.

Despite being recruited for your talent, some businesses may marginalize your greatest assets and your ambitions may exceed their vision. There may be situations in which your ideas and recommendations are heard yet not supported due to the unfamiliarity of the change proposed and their comfort level in the status quo. In these situations, you must determine if the culture of the business and how it operates would help or hinder your career goals and development. Pace varies from business to business; however, change is inevitable for all. Flexibility and patience are necessary to quickly adapt to any unfamiliar environment.

INITIAL STAFF MEETING

Once you have received and understood executive leadership's priorities and goals for your division, it is time to engage staff and find out their needs and desires. Your staff will be your primary resource for learning about the business and clientele. During staff engagements, always exude transparency and honesty, sharing privileged information on a need-to-know basis.

Before initiating any changes, observe the current practices and record all that is working well. For systems that are in place and not working well, ask questions and seek understanding as to why the current practice exists. Observe with an open mind, knowing that what worked for you in your Job A may not work in your current Job B due to business uniqueness along with other factors or information you may not be privy to at the time.

In every staff meeting, your goal is to build sustainable practices and a positive work environment. You are the coach and teammate as well. You want to create a synergistic working environment where you work with your staff and not against them. You are an advocate for your staff in senior leadership meetings, and you want to make sure that they have everything they need to get their jobs done safely and efficiently.

The first task you should complete with staff is to establish meeting rules. This is where you set the tone for the division, and it is essential that you know what you want to say and why. Be ready to answer questions and make sure everything shared has a purpose and supports your goals for the division and mission for the business. You want to share a message of positivity and love for what you do. Exude positive body language and emanate confidence for staff will be studying you and your delivery, looking for any inclination of a façade or weakness. Use nametags for meetings and try to secure a space that is large enough for all to sit comfortably.

Rules should encourage respectful behaviors that include not interrupting others when they are speaking, not using negative nonverbal communication such as eye-rolling and eye-cutting, avoiding deep sighs that indicate boredom, restlessness, or frustration, not using a cell phone or browsing a magazine or other literature, and not performing tasks irrelevant to the business such as correcting facial makeup or hair, knitting, or slyly participating in unauthorized juvenile games, conversations, and notebook doodling. You must adjust and document all unprofessional and disrespectful behavior as soon as it is observed. Elicit input from your team in establishing meeting and division rules. Staff participation can increase acceptance, buy-in, and overall adherence.

SUCCESSIVE STAFF MEETINGS

Meeting frequency can change often and depends on the business and the responsibilities of your division. Understand that production usually ceases whenever staff is in meetings, or it may lead to adverse effects in other areas of the business. Staff engagement and participation during meetings is vital to creating a positive work environment and should be a performance measure on annual staff evaluations.

In each meeting, you want to share the goals from leadership and progress made toward those goals, list areas for improvement, receive staff concerns, and end on a positive note with kudos and other acknowledgments for jobs well done. Always speak positively and encouragingly to staff. You want everyone to develop an "I can" attitude that will yield desirable results conducive to the successful and positive work environment you want to have. Avoid using negative contraction words such as "don't," "can't," "shouldn't," and "wouldn't" excessively during normal address. These words could subconsciously place unwarranted limitations on team zeal and cohesiveness and possibly breed antagonizing efforts in poorly coached staff. Positivity should dominate each meeting. Do not allow pessimism to influence action or inaction. Solicit ideas from your staff on how to improve matters that affect all, and make sure no one criticizes what others say as it could lead to disengagement. You want staff to feel empowered after each meeting, have respect for one another, and support the mission of the business.

Incorporate general facts and/or deficient findings that support the purpose and goals of the division. Clearly define benchmarks and review progress with a measurable chart or other display that is posted in a place for all to easily see. When soliciting ideas, make sure staff understand that not all opinions can be used but will be retained for another time, if needed. Always end the meeting commending everyone for their participation, and show gratitude for their hard work and efforts toward the success of the division.

CUSTOMER SERVICE

Never stop emphasizing to your staff the importance of valuing the customer and making them the priority. Make sure that all of your division efforts are designed to offer timely service without compromising quality, enhance the customer experience with a welcoming smile and helpful demeanor, and ensure the customer is comfortable at all times and someone is available to answer their questions. All staff is responsible for delivering excellent customer service and exuding a professional and positive workplace attitude. The business may also enhance the customer experience with amenities such as free refreshments and Wi-Fi, television, magazines, parking validation, and discounts on other services not offered at the business but provided by your partners. Customers are more likely to return and refer others to your business if they feel valued and are given their deserved attention.

SETTING BOUNDARIES

Once goals have been established and shared with staff, you must develop a plan of action that addresses the business's major concerns, improves the customer experience, and increases productivity. Initiating plans of action can sometimes require a change in behavior, which could be tough for staff used to the old way of doing things and who disagree with all that is proposed. So, it is imperative that you have established boundaries and core values beforehand that will dictate how staff is to interact with one another and the customer. Whenever staff steps outside of these boundaries, you must address promptly and take the necessary steps to correct the behavior. Coaching staff is an important part of the job that establishes the positive, professional, and productive work environment that everyone deserves. If you falter in holding staff accountable for outlying behaviors, you are fragmenting the foundations you wish to build upon to meet your goals.

The meetings' rules were the first set of boundaries established, and they should be used to set the boundaries outside of meetings as well. Prohibit staff from eye-rolling and sucking teeth to express objection or dislike of others and directives. Staff shouldn't gossip, raise their voice toward other staff and customers, nor argue with the customer. These may sound like common sense boundaries, but, unfortunately, they are all too familiar when working with adults.

No matter how small the infraction or infrequency, you must address it every single time and adequately coach. Failing to do so will allow the behavior to progress into much worse, especially if the person has ulterior motives to antagonize your team-building efforts and success. These efforts are a result of staff wanting things to remain the same or return to what they consider normal. When holding staff accountable for their behaviors, you are documenting what was done and following the appropriate steps of discipline to curb and correct. Treat everyone fairly with consistency and you will begin to collectively gain respect, understanding, and support from the team. Everyone deserves to work in a harmonious work environment, and you can't allow poorly coached staff to influence the behaviors of other staff through pressure and bullying tactics. Be wary of all private staff meetings, as they could be recruitment efforts to build numbers to antagonize your efforts and proposed change. These meetings usually host gossip corners and are contradictive to team cohesiveness. You want to promptly break up these meetings and assign work to prevent internal armies being formed against you. Constantly show your presence, exercise your authority in a productive way, and share your expectations.

Pay attention and take note of individual staff body language. If you pass or speak to someone in the halls and observe negative nonverbal communication, you want to spend more time with them or schedule a time to address what was observed. Not all staff will readily volunteer information or request a meeting to discuss their concerns in private. Automatically schedule periodic personal meetings with all staff. Discuss their issues if they have any and voice your concerns over negative body language. If the staff member acknowledges what you say in agreement, be sure to document their response as to why they may have expressed themselves in such a way. Unfortunately, not all staff issues outside of work remain outside. There are those who are inherently unhappy, and they bring a lot of negativity to work. Usually, the people that are dissatisfied with everything around them are mostly unhappy with themselves. During your one-on-one staff meetings, share your expectations and why it's important to the business. Make sure that employees refusing to be courteous and cordial after coaching have it reflected in their annual performance review as an area in need of improvement. All staff should be team players and contribute positivity to the workplace. Failing to address any negative behaviors will shine light on your inconsistency, and other staff may begin to distrust your leadership. Unhappy staff will always attempt to influence the opinion and actions of newer and weaker staff whose only goal is to fit in and not draw negative attention to them or be ostracized. Unhappy staff will recruit others to share their sentiment and feel justified in their actions when they can continually garner an audience.

Argumentative and belligerent behavior should not be tolerated and entertained. As manager, what you say goes, and you shouldn't engage in back-and-forth conversations with subordinates rationalizing a decision made in effort to encourage their acceptance. As long as your directives support the mission of the business, don't violate any rules or laws, and don't put anyone at risk of injury or harm, the staff member should only be concerned with the timeframe in which you want the directive completed. Investigate any directives that weren't followed and document accordingly in the staff member's record, making sure it is included in their annual performance review. You don't want to create an environment in which staff feels empowered to dispute, challenge, or question the directives you've made without consequence. It's insubordinate behavior that shouldn't be tolerated.

Unprofessional comments, inappropriate jokes, and unwanted sexual advances and gifts should all be addressed appropriately and documented. Refer to your human resources division or employee handbook if uncertain about the appropriate mode of action to take. Serious offenses may warrant immediate dismissal.

Prohibit staff from touching the belongings of others without the owner's permission. Staff should not speak negatively about the business in front of the customer. Staff should also refrain from making insensitive remarks about the customer's odor, illness, or child's appearance, or make comments with intentions to demean or poke fun at the customer's expense. Failure to hold staff accountable will lead to more bad behavior, negative business reviews, lack of team cohesiveness, and workplace disharmony.

Boundaries pertaining to leave requests prevent abuse and staff from creating unnecessary stress on daily operations. Ensure that staff follows the proper protocols for requesting vacation leave, using sick leave, and requesting overtime. Don't allow anyone to take leave or work overtime without your prior approval, and consider denying all last-minute leave requests that aren't emergent and ill-timed. The business must have adequate coverage in the absence of staff and enough time to prepare. Document all scheduled leave on one source that is visible for all employees to review daily, and be sure that all are aware that you're the only one able to alter it. Enforce proper protocol for vacation leave requests, and anyone that fails to show for duty under the pretenses that they forgot or thought they followed the proper protocols should be written up or given a verbal warning if it's their first offense.

Be attentive to staff that may selfishly abuse sick leave. These inconsiderate practices result in unnecessary stress on remaining staff and have adverse effects on operation flow for the day. To combat this abusive behavior, require that staff bring in a doctor's note in situations when their sick leave coincides with a denied leave request or when it is used to extend an already approved leave request or holiday weekend. You also want to document when staff calls in sick on a Monday or Friday and look for patterns of abuse. If a doctor's note cannot be produced in any of these mentioned situations, you must write them up to curb the undesirable practice.

COACHING STAFF

It is imperative that leaders stay vigilant and immediately address situations not conducive to a positive work environment. Often, staff will get too friendly and familiar with one another, causing professionalism to sometimes fall by the wayside. Whenever an infraction is incurred, always address the problem and not the person. Identify the problem at hand and tell the staff why it is a problem. Afterward, express the change of behavior you would like to see, and document all that was discussed in the form of a verbal warning or write-up.

The write-up is the most essential tool supervisors could use to coach staff and eliminate unwanted behaviors. Holding staff accountable for their actions disallows poorly coached individuals from passing the blame to others, and it minimizes the chances of manipulative behaviors being used in effort to avoid punishment. Accountability strengthens the workplace environment and brings awareness to the rules, expectations, and mission of the business. Staff will generally respond in a positive way when they are coached fairly and in a consistent manner.

Unfortunately, there will be staff who have never learned to function in a professional environment and adjusting to behaviors unfamiliar to them will be difficult. Rather than respond positively to coaching recommendations and improve their poor behaviors, these individuals will interpret the coaching as an expression of dislike toward them or an attack on their personal character. Staff that misinterprets coaching may become angry and start challenging or undermining your authority. If they feel their job is threatened by the coaching, staff may try to deflect attention away from them by highlighting the faults of other staff, yourself, and the business. Poorly coached staff do not enjoy being held accountable and will bring up the faults of others as well as situations in which you were inconsistent in your coaching and holding others accountable. Remember to remain focused on the coaching at hand and not be easily distracted. An employee's negative response to coaching can hinder

team cohesiveness and endanger their job and liveli-
hood. Take heed, however, to their concerns about any
coaching inconsistencies they feel are unfair.

If you fail to consistently coach staff, it will allow
disgruntled staff to express themselves in ways to make
you feel as miserable as them. Initially, they will begin
to antagonize you with subtle passive-aggressive behaviors that will progressively worsen with each coaching
session. As they sink more and more into their own
transgressions, their efforts will gradually intensify and
include varying degrees of indirect and cynical communication. There will be strategically placed sticky notes
or other signage containing barbed messages. They will
attest their need for religious support to help get them
through tough times due to difficulty experienced at
work. They will involve other staff in overt conversations and discussions they have on social media posts
with like-minded individuals sharing their sentiments.

As increased coaching encourages these staff to
improve their behaviors, they will reciprocally increase
their antagonistic efforts. To build their personal case
against you, they will begin to bad-mouth your abilities
and skills behind your back in effort to tarnish your
reputation with other staff and customers; however, the
onus is on them to prove what they say is true, and

no one will easily accept their mendacity if you have a strong intrapersonal foundation and good work ethic. This attempt to tarnish your reputation is a tactic that manipulators use to garner support, make their problems become everyone else's, and create discord. As the supervisor, don't allow these individuals to dictate your attitude because their continual poor behavior is an indication that their time with the business is coming to an end. It is utterly important that you consistently document and properly coach them whenever they step outside of your established boundaries.

As their pushback continually fails, new dastardly measures will be made for seeking your removal or hoping you'd be punished to the extent their job is preserved. Lies will be fabricated and shared with your superiors about rule-breaking, targeting and bullying staff, and other performed unprofessional behaviors they feel can't be ignored and must be addressed. As their termination becomes imminent and no other options have helped their situation, expect the ultimate attempt to save their job by feigning a medical or family emergency or intentionally injuring themselves on the job. As supervisor, you will have to weather many storms and ride many emotional roller coasters designed by poorly coached staff. With preparedness, professionalism, and consistency, you will weather them successfully without compromising team morale.

You want to minimize the influence antagonizing staff have on the rest of the team by teaching others how to handle various situations the outlier may present. Periodically schedule one-on-one meetings with all staff so that they can voice their concerns and opinions in private. Not everyone is comfortable speaking in front of a group; many prefer to remain quiet out of the fear of antagonizing the perceived general opinion of the group or they become afraid of what others may think of them. It takes real courage to antagonize the status quo and chance the unknown. However, in an intimate and private setting, most staff will share their actual opinions and will be inclined to speak more freely and honestly.

People are inherently supportive of one another and many do so even in the presence of uncertainty, self-doubt, and with limited information. When people aren't directly involved in a situation and matters don't affect them, they are more inclined to trust what is said from those in an authoritative position, those that exude the most passion, or those that successfully persuade others that their problem belongs to them as well. Unfortunately, courteousness can work against the supervisor when it comes to an unhappy staff member. Unhappy staff usually finds and ambushes another team member to vent their frustrations. While the unsuspecting staff member often blindly listens to help calm down these excited emotions, their silence and attention, however, is often misinterpreted as support. This unreal support due to courtesy often encourages a future return and episode. Recurring venting sessions by unhappy staff to unwilling audiences will have insidious repercussions if unaddressed. If supervisors aren't teaching staff how to properly handle situations concerning unhappy team members, they risk having more staff sharing the same sentiment as the staff that is disgruntled. Then one unhappy staff becomes two, and before you know it, a ripple becomes a tsunami of you versus them. Staff working synergistically against you must be coached individually so that you can share your expectations, knowledge, and understanding of their concerns.

During individual staff meetings, you want to first receive the staff member's concerns to show that their issues matter. Once shared, relate how their concerns may or may not be in line with the mission of the business and current goals. If you work long enough, you may hear staff of various businesses echo that they enjoy their job and what they do; however, the people they work with are what make it a challenge. It is important that supervisors maintain an environment in which staff can work peacefully and respectfully with one another and all have an understanding of your expectations of them. The issues that one staff is experiencing doesn't have to become the problem of others and create a negative atmosphere. Teach staff how to ask the seven questions below of their disgruntled peers so they can focus on their work with peace of mind:

- What's wrong and why do you feel the way that you do?

- What do you think you can do to improve your situation?

- Why do you think the decision you're upset with was made?

- If you were the supervisor, how would you have handled the situation differently?

- Can you see any benefit from the decision that was made?

- What are your current goals with the behavior and actions you're exuding, and what do you hope to gain?

- Have you tried speaking to the supervisor about your issue?

If staff were trained to ask these questions of their unhappy peers, those venting are least likely to bring their issues to the doorsteps of others and can possibly resolve their own issues more quickly. Staff are either unhappy with one another or the supervisor, and it's important not to ignore or take lightly their ability to form alliances that antagonize you and can create discord in the workplace. Pull these staff members aside as soon as you can and ask the same questions before problems grow too large.

Supervisors should treat each situation independent of the last and not allow past issues to negatively influence the decision-making of a present issue. This will allow individual staff growth and a stronger, more positive business atmosphere. Always remain fair and consistent because inconsistency could be used against you. Staff disgruntled due to a write-up or poor performance review can charge you with bullying, retaliation, or targeting due to personal dislike.

PROBLEM-SOLVING

A problem is anything that creates an adverse effect with how the business operates, the services offered, or the product produced. Like fingerprints, problems may resemble but they are uniquely different because of the people involved. Many problems arise due to a misunderstanding or misinterpretation of shared information while others are influenced by ignorance, actions guided by misinformation, poor work ethic, and the lack of personal integrity to do what is right for the business. There is always an available solution to any problem; however, as supervisor, you must choose the best option that produces the best outcome. Be sure to take into special consideration the current business goals, available resources, and available time. A higher level of ignorance present when solving a problem will yield you higher levels of failures and poor solutions, missed opportunities, and closed doors.

Do not allow intrapersonal issues to cloud good judgment and negatively influence your decision-making. Internal noise must be quelled before situations could be fairly and effectively addressed. In many cases, you will not have all of the facts, but it's important that the decisions you make are done with a clear head and high level of confidence that benefits the business.

In a small business, a problem can arise within the day-to-day operations or how the business is run and between personnel, which has the ability to negatively affect everything. Operational problems also affect how the product is produced and delivered for profit, and personnel problems involve the staff and their interactions with one another and the customer. When addressing a problem, always use the mission and current goals as guidance.

There are four basic steps to follow when solving operational problems. First, you must identify the problem and determine its importance at the time of discovery. It's important to understand what makes it a problem and what effects it has on the business, how much it has grown since discovery, who is responsible for it, and where and how fast it is likely to spread if action isn't taken. Concern yourself with only the facts and conduct a thorough investigation. The more accurate the information gathered, the greater the solutions and outcomes will be. Problems that don't significantly compromise the mission and goals of the business may not necessarily need immediate attention but can still worsen and should be remedied as soon as possible.

The second step to solving a problem is to specifically define your desired outcome and devise a plan to achieve. Sometimes working backward from your desired outcome can help, but it depends on the problem. Be sure your goals include a timeline for completion, responsibilities of staff, and a means for measuring progress. The more significant the problem, the more parts it may require. Be optimistic because anything is achievable with the right attitude.

Third, identify all available resources and determine which additional resources need acquiring. Resources include items such as staff, funds, equipment and supplies, and time. Secure as many resources as possible, and prioritize them according to when they are most needed in your plan in Step 2. This way you will know when each resource is needed most at a given time and those needed soon.

Finally, develop your first plan of action, using a systematic approach to stop the progression of the existing problem and establish practices to prevent its recurrence. This plan should also include measures for correcting the residual effects of the problem. If the customer, business partner, or staff were adversely affected by the problem, making proper amends will maintain a positive image of the business and protect its reputation of quality and caring service.

Personnel problems create the most discord in a business due to inconsiderate and unprofessional behaviors by poorly coached staff. These problems often lower team morale and have the potential to create a hostile environment if handled improperly. Staff involved in personnel problems often exude a wide range of emotions that are sometimes unpredictable and surprisingly excessive. To prevent this discord from happening, it is important that businesses have, in addition to established workplace boundaries, a set of core values for all to abide by and maintain. A business without core values risks lowering their bar of professionalism because there is nothing in place for which to hold staff behavior accountable. Professionalism is also compromised whenever a business cannot trust its employee(s) to do the job expected of them in a responsible and respectable way.

Due to the imperfection of humans, there will forever be a personnel issue in the workplace. Consistent coaching through disciplinary action, however, will prevent personnel issues from getting out of hand with expressed emotions that compromise the professionalism of the business. Neutralize all highly emotional situations with a calm demeanor and unwavering spirit. Promptly address any unprofessional behavior that is not conducive to a positive work environment. This may require that you take an upset staff member creating workplace disharmony to your office and have them take a seat. It is important that you have them be seated because they aren't as emotionally charged when seated as they would be standing. The more expressive a person is allowed to become and make a scene with bodily theatrics, the more likely they are to unsettle your thinking and focus and influence your decision-making. Your demeanor should only suggest neutrality. Speak calmly and avoid distractive body language and subtle facial expressions that send messages. If emotional staff interprets your nonverbal communication in a negative way, it could increase their anger and emotional level and generate feelings of distrust, unfairness, and betrayal.

Personnel problems that are one-sided are often resolved without the request of the supervisor's intervention. If staff requests you to intervene in a trivial issue they are having with another staff, determine the relevance of the issue and ask if they'd like for a meeting to be scheduled with them, you, and the other staff for a conflict resolution. If the issue is deemed important and needing immediate attention, then schedule a meeting regardless of what the staff may want so that it could be properly addressed. Not all personnel problems need immediate attention, and it is okay to delay your response and follow up with staff at a later yet reasonable time. Sometimes staff may resolve their own personnel problem when you revisit them. Nevertheless, do a follow-up to understand how the personnel problem was resolved, and ask meaningful questions to make sure it was done in a reasonable way that would prevent future occurrence. Record your follow-up efforts and the results in the staff's chart.

Whenever multiple staff come to you expressing concern or complaining about the other, schedule a meeting for all parties involved for a conflict resolution. Conflict resolution involves first identifying the problem, allowing both sides to share their side of the story, then everyone coming to a mutually agreeable solution. You have the final say with how an issue is resolved and the responsibility to hold staff accountable for the chosen resolution.

When researching the cause of a personnel problem, never develop a resolution without having a full understanding of the issue and considering all of the facts. Once a resolution is developed, it is important to effectively communicate the message to involved staff and gain bilateral understanding and acceptance. The supervisor has the ultimate responsibility to ensure staff receive and interpret information as intended. Repetition and paraphrasing the same message may be necessary to increase the understanding for some staff.

Unfortunately, staff behaviors are unpredictable. Those outside of the established workplace boundaries must always be promptly addressed due to their nature of compromising the professionalism, mission, and/or values of the business. If two staff are arguing in a public space, request that they immediately go behind closed doors. Afterward, offer mediation and document the involved staffs' responses, making them aware of your expectations and how their behaviors affect the ideals of the business. If abusive language, verbal threats, or physical contact is made, write up the violating staff member and follow up with your human resources division on the necessary next step.

Poorly coached staff will not always conduct themselves professionally and will often behave like unsupervised, mischievous children. If you delay addressing their outlying behaviors, you risk missing the opportunity for effective coaching, making it likely for the unwanted behavior to recur. Inconsistent coaching and coaching delayed for too long will only encourage staff to challenge more established boundaries. Addressing behaviors too late allows the details surrounding the event to be conveniently forgotten by the involved staff member or give them enough time to successfully use an artifice backed by a dishonest alibi to justify what was done or redirect your attention to another issue. Poorly coached staff is insensible about the effect their behaviors have on the business and fellow staff and will continue their impenitence if they are not held accountable.

Supervisors must be able to quickly identify evasive tactics used to avoid disciplinary action such as changing of the subject, highlighting an issue concerning another staff member, playing the victim to draw empathy and leniency, or flipping the blame to you or another staff because of their inability to do their job due to some erroneous reason. Be wary of any volunteered information staff may share and you did not seek during their coaching. Staff compelled to share unimportant details or opinions about others do so to aid their outcomes or support their future aspirations and hidden agendas. Though these claims may be unfounded, always record what was said, who said it, and when it was said in both staff's files. When coaching, be clear about what you witnessed the employee do, explain how it doesn't fit within the ideals of the business, and share your expectations of them for the future.

The write-up is the best way to coach an employee and correct poor behaviors. If consistently used, it will serve as a means to remove poor employees. If responsible staff is written up, they normally become upset with themselves and make the necessary changes to improve a behavior. However, irresponsible and poorly coached staff will often become indignant and make temporary improvements until their next infraction. Remain consistent with your coaching because poorly coached staff unsusceptible to improvement will continue to behave unfavorably if they aren't being held accountable for stepping outside of your established boundaries.

There are many behaviors that can compromise a professional environment and tarnish customer relations. Staff tardiness and abandonment of their duties are common behaviors that can create dissention amongst other staff and have other adverse effects on the business. You want to address any staff that habitually comes in late. Don't allow them to use vacation leave to replace missed time on their timesheets due to their tardiness. Once staff clocks in, they should begin working and everyone should have something to do. This isn't the time to make coffee, read the newspaper, browse social media outlets, eat breakfast, or do their hair and makeup. Even during downtimes, employees can be productive. Maintain a list of in-house tasks employees can complete such as wiping down the equipment and windows, checking for expired items, completing appointment confirmations or follow-up courtesy calls, and completing online training. There are many tasks staff can complete when the business isn't busy, and if you can't think of any, conduct individual meetings or perform team-building exercises. You can also ready your staff for an inspection or review emergency protocols and practice emergency scenarios. If there really is no work to be done, then allow staff to use their leave and go home early.

Supervisors should know the general whereabouts of their staff at all times and what they're doing. Staff should not be constantly taking breaks to converse with one another in back offices while customers are present nor leave their duty area to converse with staff in other departments and areas of the business. If a staff member leaves the duty area, they should notify you or make someone aware of their location in their absence. Staff that abuse allotted breaks or desert their duty station should be coached and have it reflected in their performance reviews if it persists.

It is important that staff individuality is left at home and they conform to the standards established by the business when they arrive for work. Having uniforms or a dress code are simple ways to limit individuals from expressing themselves at work. If you decide to have a dress code, then include as many specifics as possible that address how clothing should fit, the colors and patterns allowed or disallowed, how much skin is allowed to show, and which styles, colors, size, designs, and how tight they are allowed to be. Stipulations should extend to accessories as well and include acceptable eyewear and jewelry styles, hairstyles, perfume intensity, and tattoo visibility. It is unprofessional for staff to express themselves at work as they would in their homes and in their private lives. If professionalism is compromised, customers may not have the confidence to return to your business or refuse to recommend others to it.

Staff may also express themselves through music and television programming. If music is played in the office, avoid stations that play offensive and vulgar songs and those that are radio talk shows sharing opinions and gossip. Also, avoid television channels that host the same type of programming along with channels that show violence, have controversial and inappropriate subject matter, or those that can create ill feelings and emotions. These programming can be highly offensive to the customer and even other staff by creating an unprofessional working environment.

Supervisors should also place limitations on when and where staff could use their cell phones. Disallow staff to keep their personal phones in their pockets and prohibit use of cell phones any place other than the break room and outside in the parking lot away from customers. Curb these behaviors with proper coaching, warning, and a write-up if necessary. It's highly unprofessional for a customer to not be greeted and helped until after the staff member finishes using their mobile device or other electronic.

As supervisor, you will experience irrational, unreasonable, and very wrong customers that will take issue with hardworking staff. In these situations, you must advocate for your employee and defend them and their hard work against anyone who speaks to the contrary. Encourage staff to always remain professional even in the midst of belligerent and combative customers, and instruct them to walk away if they are victims of customer verbal abuse. The supervisor must quell these tempers and rectify the situation, making sure to follow up with the involved staff member. Commend staff that handled the situation properly and maintained their professionalism until the issue was resolved. The customer also has the responsibility to behave properly in your business and should be made aware that their behaviors are not conducive to the professional environment you're trying to maintain. Invite unhappy customers into a private office or space away from other customers, investigate their issue, and get them the proper help. If they remain belligerent, then ask them to leave the business premises. If they refuse, initiate security for their removal. Staff responds best to supervisors that are consistent and predictable, and they feel that their best interests are at hand.

MISTAKES

A mistake is defined as a wrong judgment or action. In business, however, a mistake is failing to do something that you were supposed to do while having the proper awareness. When a supervisor makes a decision and takes action based on the information received, it is not necessarily a mistake if the results are unfavorable. Outcomes always improve with new and better information and what was learned from an initial course of action. Mistakes in business are purposeful actions made due to forgetfulness or with intention due to the knowledge that the consequences present a favorable balance between the benefit and cost/risk.

When staff is affected by a supervisor's mistake in an emotional, physical, or financial way, it's important that supervisors be honest about their mistake and offer a sincere apology to salvage team cohesiveness and morale. Often, the mistake is unintentional and due to a supervisor forgetting something for which they were responsible. Before apologizing, the supervisor must acknowledge and agree that they've made a mistake and then accept the responsibility to make amends and correct. A sincere apology requires an appropriate tone of voice and proper inflection along with body language of concern. Apologies must be sincere and compassionate and never end with the word "but" followed by an excuse justifying why the mistake was made. The use of "but" after an apology invalidates the sincerity of the apology and shares the message that you really aren't sorry and not taking responsibility for the mistake. It is an attempt to gain sympathy and understanding from the victim you wronged so that you can feel better about yourself.

Once an apology is made, you should follow up with a solution for how to rectify the situation and prevent it from happening again. After these steps are completed, it is okay to move forward and let it go because you owe them nothing else. Moving forward means not allowing anyone to dwell on your past mistake and keep it fresh in your mind when you have already corrected and moved past it. If, however, the same mistake is repeated, then your initial solution for prevention wasn't good enough and something different needs to be done.

CHAPTER 3

ESTABLISHING PRACTICES FOR BUSINESS LONGEVITY

Many unpredictable factors can significantly influence the longevity of a business. It is important that, as supervisor, you know the longevity goals and expectations of the owner or founder of the business and determine how they fit within your career aspirations. The owner usually sets the lifespan goals of the business before its inception and has them closely related to their financial goals and responsibilities to their family. The more you understand where the business is in relation to their goals, the better informed you can be about pursuing the opportunity. Because a business is most likely to fail within their first five years of existence, supervisors must also determine if the owner has a clear vision and realistic expectations and is investing adequate effort and sacrifice for the business to succeed. Small businesses are unpredictable and not many continue beyond the owner's retirement or death. Your outcome then becomes dependent on the decisions of the descendants or new owners who may now choose to go in a different direction that doesn't include you.

Other factors to consider when determining the longevity of a business are the present demand for the product produced or service being offered, strength of the business's competitors, quality and commitment of staff and leadership, and the business's ability to change with the times and adapt to new consumer demands. The most relevant factor to business longevity, however, is how much the business invests in its employees. Investing in an employee's growth and well-being makes them feel valued and rewarded. Businesses can offer their employees many intangibles that will yield optimal performance, pride, and dedication.

As mentioned earlier, there are no limits to the wants of an employee. With each acquisition and relinquishment, a new want will appear until it evolves into getting more for doing less. Though it is a privilege to have a job, businesses should understand the needs and priorities of their employees, and seek ways to meet their employees' needs without forcing the employee to make significant financial or familial sacrifice. The supervisor's responsibility to ensuring longevity is to acknowledge and reward the employee's hard efforts and performance and give compassionate and consistent supervision.

Building Leaders

It's important that businesses invest in employee training opportunities to help their staff reach their fullest potential. The more skills and talents that individual employees possess often translates into success and longevity for the business. Supervisors aren't readily aware of staff weaknesses, and not many staff will volunteer the information. As such, the supervisor must be vigilant and listen for phrases or responses such as "we can't," which usually means that they don't know how, or "that's just the way it is," which usually translates into their never considering another option because the current way is how they learned it. Supervisors must investigate and question everything that doesn't add up or make any sense and fails to offer a justification for its existence.

As supervisor, you want to build a culture of "we can" amongst staff and encourage them to find a way to accomplish any task presented to them. Businesses with properly trained staff are able to quickly troubleshoot and identify roadblocks, understand their origins, and formulate several solutions to remedy the situation to reach their goal. In contrast, disempowered and undertrained staff will fail to address an issue at its inception or, once identified, fail to make others aware until the issue worsens and possibly lead to additional problems. Usually, undertrained staff works only within their comfort zones and lacks proper knowledge of available resources they could use to make their jobs easier. They are less than thrilled about being part of a team that works together. Only through staff investment and encouragement can the best of staff be brought out for the benefit of the business.

Begin building and teaching staff by engaging them and seeking their input on different issues that are familiar to them. Then, put staff in unfamiliar situations in which they have to use the problem-solving steps to produce a meaningful solution. Involve yourself only when necessary. Be aware of what's being done and make sure all understand the need for your acceptance of the final solution. If staff is having difficulty learning something new, have someone experienced demonstrate the process and provide the staff member with written step-by-step directions of the process for later review whenever they need it. To ensure complete understanding, have the staff member complete the task as much as possible and give them the responsibility of training new staff on the process afterward. If speed is an issue for a staff member due to age or disability, find a position or situation where it wouldn't matter and is preferable that they go slow and not rush. Place staff in positions where they can grow and be proficient.

Businesses thrive when employees are put in positions of success, encouraged to share their ideas for improvement, and given proper support. Enthused staff is focused on what they can contribute to the business, and this excitement often sparks ingenuity. Businesses want to avoid extinguishing staff excitement and discouraging their involvement in doing what's best for the business. Allow staff to share their ideas to prevent them from feeling undervalued. Not all of their ideas will be great, but it won't hurt to listen. Supervisors must engage their staff and give positive feedback. When staff shares useful ideas, tell them how important their recommendation is to the business and the positive effect it will have on the customer and society. Individual staff success will matriculate into team and business success and longevity. Be sure that their staff involvement and positive behaviors are reflected positively in their performance review.

When staff does well, praise them in front of everyone, especially if the task completed was non-routine and had a positive impact on the mission. Periodically inquire about the needs of your staff and anything you can do to help them perform optimally or do their jobs better. Do your best to obtain these staff requests and follow up with them if an item cannot be procured. Acknowledging staff effort helps to build their self-confidence and increases overall morale.

Immense flexibility is an absolute requirement for businesses to successfully adapt to change. Change is an inevitable force of nature that has the ability to inhibit progress and shorten longevity by presenting new or unfamiliar situations that sometimes require immediate adjustments and behavior changes by everyone. As businesses grow, new laws made, and technologies advance, policies and procedures will have to adapt and reflect the best practices that support the mission and goals of the business. Staff doesn't always welcome change and many would often default to antiquated practices at the first sign of trouble, questioning the relevance and effectiveness of the new requirements. Inflexibility is a mindset that needs constant encouragement for those unaccepting of or having difficulty adapting to change.

Opinions about change usually support what an individual knows best, and their actions are normally guided by that which they are accustomed. Only time and consistent accountability for the new requirements can influence opinion. It is a natural process for views to evolve and produce internal harmony with newly required behaviors. Insisting that someone change their views before they are ready will only breed immediate hostility and resentment. Supervisors must concern themselves only with the behaviors and not the sentiment of staff.

Many decisions will be made by leadership without the staff's ability to provide input. This lack of having a voice or proper representation usually breeds an unwanted uncertainty and pessimism amongst staff that can adversely affect team performance. A supervisor's role during these situations is to be a liaison between staff and leadership, a voice of reason to help minimize staff's mental anguish due to their inability to influence decisions pertinent to them. It is important for the supervisor to support all changes recommended by leadership wholeheartedly, understand its purpose and how it supports the mission, and tackle designated responsibilities together with your staff. When relaying these messages to staff, use open communication, encourage staff acceptance, and share a clear message with utter transparency.

It is important that the supervisor exudes daily an enthusiastic and dedicated persona conducive of one that takes pride in their work and the business. If your true sentiment is to the contrary, then you must never share it with others within the business, especially your subordinates. Always remember to lead by example and maintain an environment of positivity. Ill feelings shared by anyone in a leadership position about the business will stir ill feelings experienced by others and decrease team morale. Employees that feel undervalued will focus their attention on all they consider negative and unfair within the business and aim to create unrest within others. As supervisor you must encourage them not to ignore the positive aspects of the job and at the same time advocate for them if they have a valid argument. Despite the validity of some of their concerns, a supervisor's role is to minimize the influence they have on other staff. Sometimes supervisors have to find creative ways to motivate, inspire, and placate staff in an effort to add value where you deem it missing.

Accolades and recognition for jobs well done are very meaningful to staff and can have lingering positive effects on morale and performance. Constantly express appreciation to staff for their hard work and surprise them with an occasional fruit tray, pastry tray, or box of chocolates to say thank you. Staffs that feel valued are least likely to seek better opportunities at another business and spread bad words about your business. Be sure to invest in your staff, listen to them, and advocate for them, and they will be more receptive and flexible to proposed change and help prolong the longevity of the business.

Unique Benefits

Demographically, there are generally three types of employees with unique needs that can represent almost all employees: those that are single and childless, those with small children, and the empty nester or soon-to-be empty nester with college-age children. They represent the life cycle of an employee, and each period or phase generally has a different set of priorities. The employee that is single and childless usually has no real commitments, and their main focus is usually money and making as much as they can. Those with children are concerned with salary but also medical insurance for the family, annual leave and holiday time off, and other familial benefits. Employees in the latter one-third of their careers are usually more focused on their health and retirement benefits. Businesses that cater to the accurate phase and priorities of their employees increase the likelihood of that employee engaging and giving their best to the business. These unique benefits may include childcare perks, flexible working hours, four-day work week with full-time being 32 hours, discount entertainment and food vouchers, and bonuses for excellent performance. As life situations change, so will staff priorities; many begin to understand that there is more to life than money, and it is hard to find happiness when they are working and not living. Reaching retirement isn't a guarantee for anyone, and for those lucky to reach retirement, mobility isn't guaranteed. When a business can improve the quality of life of their employees and help them enjoy and secure useful benefits now without forcing on them what isn't needed or is unwanted, they are indirectly investing in their own longevity. Cookie-cutter benefit packages do not always meet the needs of all staff unless they are unquestionably outstanding. Unique benefits that cater to individual needs show staff they are valued.

As an employee approaches retirement, it would benefit the business to have a progressive exit plan for those that have been with the business for the entirety of their career. These seasoned employees have been through many of the ups and downs of the business and have become the unofficial face of the business to customers. They are like extended family to many they have worked with over the years, continually represent the business admirably, and serve with loyalty and dedication. This commitment to the business should warrant them favorable exits, and they should be allowed to leave on their terms. How businesses treat these employees will influence significantly the opinion, morale, and dedication of remaining staff and customers. Exit plans show true value for staff's service and allow smooth transitions for retiring staff whose abilities and skills aren't meeting the current needs of the business.

Unique benefits that are tailored to the individual can help retain current talent and increase the pool of new talent from which to choose. Despite a business's efforts to show that they value their employees, there will still be cases of employees seeking the proverbial greener pasture elsewhere. This can't be prevented and, in many cases, those that chose to leave often seek to return once they realize how much better they had it. Their experience will weigh heavily with other employees, solidify the commitment they have to the business, and discourage them from entertaining the idea of leaving as well.

ENGAGING LEADERSHIP

A business is only as strong as its leader and the team they employ to make and represent the product or provide their service. In order for a business to thrive, there needs to be a clean line of communication between leadership and its employees. The supervisor is the voice of the employee and should have a seat at the leadership table for all meetings. Any supervisor without a seat at the table is a powerless titleholder that risks their reputation being tarnished if leadership needs a scapegoat held responsible for a failure and to hide their weakness. It's important for supervisors to know the cause of any failure that occurs within their division or reason for low production. If you are unable to identify the cause of a problem within your division, you will be kept from the leadership table because of your inability to offer a solution to remedy pertinent situations. Business longevity is prolonged when leadership takes responsibility for their actions and tries not to divert attention or pass blame to others.

It would behoove any leader of a business to have adequate representation from all divisions of the business that use funds to operate and can bring in revenue. Supervisors are the only advocate for staff in leadership meetings and hold the responsibility of securing the resources their staff needs to function efficiently, safely, and at capacity. The mission and goals of the business should guide leadership, and your requests should always support the mission and cater to improving the customer experience. Find shared problems your division has with leadership, and use this information to acquire the resources that could benefit your staff.

If there are several divisions within your business, know that there is an unwritten hierarchy based on profitability and/or demand for service. Despite this fact, supervisors must work together and ensure that their staff is protected against unfair and one-sided sacrifices made during collaborations that yield no benefit to their divisions. Staff responds positively when their supervisors fight for their issues, not put the interests and agendas of others before their own. You should always view your division as the most important and convince your staff likewise.

Study the organizational chart, job descriptions, and the responsibilities for all staff within the business so that you'd know whom to contact to help you best solve an issue. Have special awareness of those with positions that directly affect you and your division. Never bypass the supervisor of another division in an effort to contact their subordinate to help you resolve an issue. Businesses thrive best when their supervisors of various divisions are respectful to one another and can work in a complementary manner. Communication and requests should always begin between supervisors, and no correspondence between them should include a subordinate unless it was mutually agreed that they be invited and are vital to your current goals. Always seek permission to use the staff of other divisions, and coach your staff to direct any supervisor to you if they need your division's assistance in a particular matter.

Interdivision communication and positive relationships with other leaders enable a supervisor to better address the issues within their division by using a multidimensional approach. It would behoove any supervisor to notify their peers within the business about an issue they're experiencing and inquire about any special considerations needed to resolve their problem. The more parts and information gathered beforehand can help resolve the issue quicker and more smoothly. Also, be aware of the potential effects resolving your issue may have on the customer and business, and be sure your immediate supervisor is made aware and has signed off on it. Take charge of issues pertinent to you and your division, and do not delegate this task to another supervisor whose competence and abilities are unproven and may lack the experience of resolving similar issues. Developing positive relationships with other supervisors and those in leadership will help improve business efficiency and prolong longevity.

The more you learn and know about the executive leadership team, the better and more effectively you can engage them. Learn as much as you can about their dynamics and the relationships they have with one another. The person with the most senior title doesn't always have the most power, and they may not be responsible for making the biggest decisions for the business. Your staff may be your most reliable resource to gather this information, but be careful with the manner of inquiry because you don't know the nature of their relationship. Avoid expressing personal opinions you have about anyone and request that others only share with you the facts. Immediately interrupt any attempts staff makes to share personal sentiments and negative opinions about leadership. If you listen and respond to meaningless information, you have engaged yourself in gossip and have failed to lead by a good example.

It's imperative that businesses keep up with the times and advancements in technology for survival. Many, unfortunately, operate behind this technological curve for various reasons and remain true to their antiquated or fledgling practices, which stagnate growth and shorten their longevity. As time progresses, businesses must reassess their priorities, and leaders must adapt to their changing environments and set bold goals to meet current customer needs and demands. Unfortunately, businesses allow past "lightning in a bottle" success of a leader to carry one's reputation beyond their expiration date because of their performance during a time of need several years ago in earlier days of the business. Businesses must prevent loyalty to leadership to supersede its mission and find ways to prolong longevity and strengthen its foundation with a new vision and bolder goals.

As a supervisor, don't allow stagnant leadership to stifle your responsibilities to the business and progress. During scheduled meetings, have a set agenda for what you wish to accomplish. If leadership meetings involve the supervisors of other divisions, only ask questions and make comments pertaining to your division. Commenting about the operations of others will only fragment relationships within the group of peers. When you speak, make sure that your message is clear, succinct, and doesn't waste time with useless information. All listeners have different perspectives and will interpret or process the information differently. Be sure to get clear and definitive answers to your questions during leadership meetings without losing focus of your meeting goals. Distractions such as praise and accolades, meaningless rambling by your supervisor, or a change of subject can refocus the attention and support of the group to the meeting goals set by others at the table.

STRATEGIC PARTNERSHIPS

Building strategic partnerships is a great way to expose your business to potential new customers and associate with other reputable businesses. These relationships can strengthen your business against competitors and lead to additional relationships with other businesses. Businesses focused on longevity are always looking for creative ways to expand services and increase products offered; customers are always looking to be told what they need or would enjoy. Strategic partnerships don't necessarily require financial investment, but both partners usually benefit from the relationship.

When forming a strategic partnership, gain permission beforehand from your immediate supervisor. This is to ensure that there are no aspects about the potential partner that could damage your business's reputation and that proper protocols are being followed when establishing the relationship. You also want to make sure there isn't a negative past history between your business and the partner and no preexisting contractual obligations that would negate the partnership. Ideally, you want to find a partner that can get your name to a wider customer base, has a reputation comparable to or greater than yours, or is trying to fulfill a philanthropic endeavor. The image of your business must be protected at all costs. If you can't visualize a potential partner representing your product or business, then you want to avoid that partnership.

Be transparent with all potential partners about your goals, needs, and expectations, and share only relevant information without any embellishment. Stay focused on the mission of your business and avoid being misguided by greed or other ignoble reason. Consider your partnership a failure if either side feels as though they've gotten the lesser end of the stick. Review partnerships annually and determine their usefulness to your business; discontinue or renegotiate those that are no longer beneficial.

Strategic partnerships should be nurtured and their representatives always welcomed to your business. It is important that you coach staff to treat all guests in a warm and personable manner. Visitors should be engaged and never ignored to the point they have to initiate the conversation for help. Encourage your staff to smile, make eye contact, and introduce themselves to anyone they haven't met. Ignoring visitors is very unwelcoming and could harness ill feelings that could strain the partnership. If roles are changed and you're the visitor, don't pretend that host staff is invisible, unimportant, or not present. You must engage your partner's staff as though you were the host to have a positive influence over the future of the relationship.

In any partnership in which you receive some sort of benefit, always be grateful and show gratitude. If money or other gift or donation are given to your business, do not fail to send a thank you note, card, or email, and follow up with a phone call. Expressed gratitude and appreciation goes a long way and may open the doors for future donations and other partnerships.

EXPANSION

The ability to expand your business is a wonderful way to reach new customers and expand the business's visibility while increasing its longevity. There are many factors you need to consider before expanding, in addition to having a market analysis beforehand. Know your product first and foremost. Is your product or the service you provide essential or nonessential? Is it a seasonal item or service or do certain geographical features limit its use? Nonessential items are usually those of leisure that a customer can do without.

During times of financial crisis or other hardship, the nonessential items and services will be the last sought, which could cause the business to suffer. However, the customer cannot do without essential items no matter how difficult the times may get. You also want to know about your competition in the area to which you're considering expanding, the timeliness of your product or service, and the cost of expansion. If you're not meeting the demands of your customers consistently while operating at maximum capacity in regards to staffing and hours of operation, then you should consider expanding your business.

There are risks that come with expansion, however; if expansion was deemed necessary, don't allow these risks to stifle your ambitions and deter what is needed. Be sure to maintain your core values and be motivated by need and not greed. Focus on serving your customer and meeting their needs. Misguided expansion efforts may lead to overexpansion and business failure. Overexpansion will require that the business cut costs through means of staff layoffs, cutting staff hours, reducing the hours of operation, decreasing the supplies purchased, or cutting back the services offered. Some businesses caught in this overexpansion predicament fail to pay their employees on time due to lack of funds. By all means, never fail to pay your employees on payday. Expand at a well-informed and controlled pace that matches your current demand.

During expansion efforts, be sure to maintain the strong foundations you've already established for yourself and the business. Be sure that current staff understands your expectations of them and their new responsibilities. If you have to recruit new staff, avoid settling for a poorer quality worker just to fill a position quicker. However, during times of desperation, get what you can get, knowing that you must coach this employee up to where you need them to be or risk having them cause a different state of desperation or depression within your team.

SIGNS OF TERMINATION

All relationships in business eventually come to an end of some sort. Hard work, dedication, and effort aren't all that is required for your job security. As an employee of the business, you must learn to understand that loyalty only goes in one direction, and results and the bottom line are valued more than an employee's history and loyalty to the business. If you are terminated, you will be replaced and the memory of your years of service and contributions forgotten. Don't take it personally because it's just the nature of business, and you won't be the last to experience it.

Depending on the type of business you work for and the goals of the owner, your power and influence over staff may be viewed as a threat to progress and to the direction new leadership wishes to take the business. If there is a transition of leadership, avoid becoming a target of dismissal by having immense flexibility, avoiding antagonizing stances, and seeking direction. Supervisors that fail to seek direction from the new leader and accommodate these new changes will eventually see their responsibilities reduced to futile tasks outside of their normal job description and duties. Termination isn't imminent at this time, but certain actions may signal the beginning of the end for you. If you are demoted to a position of lesser power and your salary decreased, your office is taken and you're allowed to work from home, your responsibilities are given to someone of less seniority, you're being passed over for a raise or promotion, you're given a bad performance review, or your contributions are limited to the business, these are all telltale signs you are no longer wanted and needed at the business. Update your resume and begin looking into a Plan B because you may have six months remaining with the business. In the meantime, continue working hard and communicate as much as you can by email for direction, clarifications, and deadlines. Record any bullying or intimidation tactics and always speak up for yourself. If you're given a bad performance review and disagree with what was said, then dispute in writing and share all that is not true, highlighting in your rebuttal areas where you have excelled in performance. Include as many facts, figures, or statistics as possible to support your case. These facts can include customer satisfaction surveys and response times, punctuality to work, case completions, money produced, attendance, etc. Do not rely on others to defend you with the fervor as you would yourself. Facts and truths are easily backed by data, whereas lies die or disappear quickly without proof.

Don't allow the dubious tactics of new leadership to increase your discontent with the business. These tactics are meant to encourage one to leave voluntarily out of the fear that their future career aspirations could be tarnished. Do your best to complete the last-minute, poorly communicated, and unfamiliar tasks with confidence and enthusiasm. Those guilty of ignoble practices are closing doors unbeknownst to them due to their unawareness of relationships that are preexistent and outside of their control. If you are on the other side of a termination and releasing a staff member, just remember to remain professional, and don't celebrate or discuss their departure with other team members.

Understanding Priorities

Driven supervisors excel in their careers because they have a meaningful and selfless purpose to do what they do. Knowing your absolute priorities in life allows you to remain focused on your responsibilities and not sweat a lot of small, unimportant stuff. Supervisors will have bad days that they must put into perspective and remember what really matters most in life. Everyone with stress welcomes it by the decisions they make. Think positively about the decisions you make because it allows you to focus on your responsibilities. Pessimistic thinking creates a bad mood and redirects your focus to your problems and how to complain rather than solve them. Allow life to happen and growth to occur. Who you are today isn't necessarily who you'll be tomorrow. Find time to legally decompress each day and enjoy all that adds meaning to your life. Take care of your health, spend time with loved ones, and politely say no once in a while.

Wherever your career takes you, know that you're in the driver's seat making the decisions. You want to be in a position in which you're choosing the job more than they are choosing you. If things don't turn out exactly how you imagined them, then take the necessary additional steps to get where you wish to be. If you're young and new in your career, never turn down an opportunity to expose yourself to a new experience or situation that won't cost you anything. Meet as many new people you can, be polite to everyone, and work well with others. Doors open and close based on your reputation and how you treat others. Never settle for less or be complacent with stagnant growth unless you are content where you are and career advancement isn't on your radar of self-achievement.

Jobs are a big part of life but not your complete life. Don't hesitate in requesting your due in salary; pursue other options if necessary. Erase self-defeatist thoughts that disguise themselves as logic and reasoning when they're generally a form of fear and self-doubt to deter you from going after what you want most. Inaction today will lead to future regret, and the fire and zeal once held will eventually fizzle out with time. Failure to grow into your own greatest expectations will open the door for you to become a minion helping others meet their greatest expectations.

Mentorship

Businesses build reputable names in their communities not only by the product they sell or service they offer but also by serving their communities and giving back. Volunteering in the community, offering shadowing opportunities for high school kids, providing internships for college kids, and mentoring young professionals are all wonderful ways businesses can give back to their communities. Creating positive experiences for youth are a sure way to get your name out in a positive way and attract talent to your business. Providing opportunities for your staff to do good for others will also add value to their jobs and allow them to hone their skills and become model employees due to their new responsibility of being a positive role model. This type of community involvement and staff pride will prolong the business's longevity because now the community wants the business to succeed and your staff wants it to thrive.

Mentorship isn't just for youth and college kids but also for staff interested in climbing the career ladder and supervisors interested in becoming better leaders. Supervisors are the unknown and unsung heroes of the world that indirectly help shape society by influencing adult behaviors and teaching staff what wasn't learned in their youth. Due to this responsibility, it is important that supervisors themselves lead by example. They must know how to work well with others and function professionally and respectfully in public places. Not all supervisors are created equal and not all are good mentors. When seeking a good mentor, first observe how well one interacts with their staff. Observe the overall atmosphere of their division. Listen to how well they communicate with their staff. Do they interact well with other leaders? How well have they engaged you, and do you think their peers and team generally respect them? Avoid supervisors that are constantly in a bad mood, complain often, speak ill of their peers and superiors, and don't have control over their divisions. Good mentors will often share thoughtful and sound advice, are reliable and never too busy, and they understand what it takes to be successful. Good mentoring will make a positive difference in anyone's life. It gives the mentee inspiration, hope, and motivation to do their best and be their best.

Anyone can be a mentor and the more you can relate to the mentee, the more you can inspire. Share personal stories, speak of your failures and accomplishments, and relate. Invest your time in those that are serious, committed to their own development, and seeking guidance. Guide the mentee based on your knowledge and all that was learned from your past experiences. Good mentors are attentive, decisive, and lead by example. You cannot be a good supervisor without being a good mentor. Encourage others to be the best they can be, and be there when they need you. The job of a supervisor is never finished because there are always responsibilities needing fulfillment. Are you ready to step up to the task of making the world a better place and establishing a professional, productive, and positive working environment for your business? If so, know that you can do it and know that a lot of people are counting on you.

Good luck!

ACKNOWLEDGMENTS

I would like to thank my mom, Lutricia, and father, Charles Sr., for their dedication to our family and continued presence. They worked hard, led by example, and provided admirably for their children. A lot of my motivation is driven by a continued desire to make them proud.

I wouldn't be where I am today without the mentorship of Dr. Dwight McMillan and Dr. Gwendolyn Brown. Dr. Dwight McMillan influenced me to become a dentist by showing a genuine interest in me each time I shadowed him during high school and college. He took his responsibility as a mentor beyond expectations and taught me the importance of how mentors can impact the lives of others. I will never forget Dr. McMillan's enthusiasm, knowledge, hustle, and ambitions. They were all contagious and inspiring.

Dr. Gwendolyn Brown is the consummate leader who taught me about maintaining workplace harmony and professionalism. She is a very tough, smart, and accomplished practitioner who is like a surrogate mother. I can always count on her to offer sound advice to help solve any workplace issue. She demands the best of everyone and makes sure that all understand their roles and expectations.

I would also like to thank Dr. Michael N. Williams and Dr. Joyce Davis for carrying the torch set by Dr. Brown and Dr. McMillan. I admire Dr. Williams' involvement in his community, willingness to help others, and, like Dr. McMillan, his hustle. Not much can slow him down whenever he is in his zone, including a torn Achilles tendon. He and his wife, Tracy, make a great team as parents, business owners, and mentors. I met Dr. Davis not long before she was due to retire. Dr. Davis is a very petite yet exceptionally tough practitioner who maintained calm in seemingly stressful situations. She carried herself with pride, said no more than necessary, and took her responsibilities seriously.

I am also grateful for my time spent in the United States Air Force. There, I learned the importance of having strong policies and abled leaders. I am also thankful to the Washington State Department of

Corrections that taught me the importance of being fair, firm, and consistent with those for whom you are responsible.

I would like to thank Maile Roubideaux, Becky Corpuz, Jenny Hernandez, and Esther Lucero of the Seattle Indian Health Board (SIHB). Jenny Hernandez, author of *The Parenting Exchange*, taught me how to focus on the situation and not the person during remediation, and Esther Lucero showed me how to establish boundaries and hold staff accountable to those boundaries. SIHB is where most of my lessons in supervision were learned and I was motivated to write this book.

I would also like to thank special friends Drs. Shannon and Sabra Slaughter. They have always welcomed me and my family into their home, and their friendship provides a certain intangible gift that inspires me to be my best yet remain humble. I have always felt a special connection with them, and I wish there was more I could do to show my appreciation.

Finally, I would like to thank my wife, Tiara, and our daughters, Madison and Camille, for their love, support, and inspiration. This book would not have been finished without them. They are a priceless gift I am blessed to have in my life.

ABOUT THE AUTHOR

DR. CHARLES I. BROWN was born and raised in Orangeburg, SC. He graduated from the College of Charleston with a degree in biology and obtained his doctorate of dental medicine degree from the Medical University of South Carolina. Dr. Brown began his dental career as an officer in the United States Air Force, serving in Omaha, NE, and Wichita, KS. After an honorable separation from the Air Force and a brief return to South Carolina, his career led to dental director positions in Seattle, WA, then Durham, NC. After completing a year sabbatical in Salamanca, Spain, he and his family relocated to Alexandria, VA.

Lightning Source UK Ltd.
Milton Keynes UK
UKHW022308120421
381888UK00010B/789/J